HAVING A Peace OF MIND

Relying Totally on God's Word

LIONEL B. PEARSON

Having A Peace of Mind

Relying Totally on God's Word

Lionel B. Pearson, Author

Published by D’Tor Publishing

P.O. Box 42816, Towson, Md. 21284

www.RWCBaltimore.Churchspring.org
DTornetwork@gmail.com

Ebook edition created 2020

Library of Congress Cataloging-in-Publication Data is on file at the Library of Congress, Washington, DC.

eBook ISBN: 978-1-7373575-1-3
Paperback ISBN: 978-1-7373575-0-6

Unless otherwise indicated, translations of ancient texts, including Scripture quotations, are the author’s translation.”

DEDICATION

To my Lord and Savior,
Jesus Christ

This Book is nothing without you. And I Dedicate it back from whence it Originally came, Haven.

&

To
My Wife:
Katrina L. Pearson
This Book is

AFFECTIONATELY DEDICATED

CONTENT

ACKNOWLEDGMENTS

~ To my parents the late Theodore A. Pearson and the present Dr. Nellie E. Pearson,

Thank you for allowing God to use you to bring forth purpose. Thank you for teaching me why it was necessary to have a relationship with God.
But mainly, I want to thank you for loving me, and teaching me the core values of life.

~ To the most Anointed Woman and Mother on the planet, Dr. Nellie E. Pearson. I Thank and Praise God for you covering me in prayer even while in your womb. And for teaching me the secret of having a relationship with God, through Salvation.

~ To my sister, Theresa and my two Amazingly Talented Nieces Dynasty and Torri,

You all put the sweet and spice that keeps your Bubba and Uncle always on the move.

~ To all my family and friends,

I want to thank and acknowledge you for being there for me when I needed you the most period.
From my heart to yours.

~ To my RWC Church Family,

What can I say?
I love all of you. Not for being apart the RWC family, that was already predestined.
I love you because, you trust the God that's in me to lead, teach and cover such a powerful nation of people such as you.

I am extremely grateful to walk this path with you.

Pastor

LET US PRAY:

Father, I want to first say, Thank you.
Thank you Master for all you have done for me. Thank you, Lord, for preparing me for this day and time to serve your people.

Secondly, I want to Thank you God for Saving my soul. Thank you for delivering me from the hands of darkness. Thank you for shielding my mind and overwhelming me with the Holy Ghost to lead and guide me all through life's test, trials, and traps.

Thank you Master for choosing and using me for this appointed time and assignment. I want to thank you for this very important opportunity for placing this word in Spirit that was and is purposely meant for your people.

Thank you, God, for birthing this resource in me, so that others can have an extended source of ammunition that will help and prepare them for their chosen assignment(s).
Thank you Master for showing me how to write this book the way that you want it to be written.

Thank you, Lord, for the faithful few that are constantly praying for me, and my assignment.

I pray Master that this word will penetrate the hearts of the oppress. That it will revive and restore the broken, rescue the lost, and redeem the prisoners of this world. I pray that through this resource lives will be instantly and consistently changed for the better.

I speak life and wholeness in the name of Jesus to whomever decides to invest in their own lives. I speak healing and deliverance in the name of Jesus. I demand that the very thing that is trying it's very best to kill you; I pray that it will fall victim to its own defile in Jesus' Mighty name.

Sister be set free. Brother be renewed by the renewing of your mind. Come out from the comfortable place of darkness and walk with your head held high by the Spirit of the Holy Ghost.

Children obey your parents in the name of Jesus so that your days maybe filled with joy.

If you are reading this prayer right now, then I pray that God will release you from the past in order that future can shine above your hurt.

I pray against that victim mentality in order that God can use you as a course of action, so that God can get the Glory and you will get the Victory.

In Jesus Name I Pray, Amen

1
Having a Peace of Mind
What is it?

January 9, 2020

Alright, so the question that resonates is this. What is a good understanding of the phrase: Having a Peace of Mind?

Having a Peace of Mind can be understood as: to maintain our *Deliverance.*

What is maintenance or to maintain?

maintain is defined as - *to keep in an appropriate condition or in operation; to keep in existence or continuance; preserve.*

"The New Combined Bible Dictionary and Concordance" Charles F. Pheifer, p. 284

My interpretation of the word **maintaining** is - *to provide for; to support, keep or to uphold what's valuable.*
To maintain means to defend it or even nurture your valuables. In other words, to maintain something, is to help our valuables to grow.

We've all at one point or another in our lives purchased something(s) that we were trying so desperately to preserve it . We thought of different ideas, we've gotten all kinds of advice from family, friends, co-workers, next door neighbor; we didn't care where the information came from, all we knew was, I've got to keep this as long as I possibly can.

Let me share this with you. When my sister and I were children, we had to play either in my room or in the basement. Very rarely were we permitted to play or horse around in the living room or dining room because, my mother did not want us to break or mess up anything, especially after she had just finished cleaning.

Now what I did not understand then was, how could we break or mess up the living room & or the dining room when my mother had these plastic slip covers over everything?

And I mean everything!!

We had plastic slip covers for the furniture. We had plastic slip covers to cover the dining room tablecloth. We had plastic slip covers for the dining room chairs. We had plastic floor runners going from the front door to the kitchen. We even had plastic floor runners going up the stairs. I mean it seem like the world of plastic would never end in our house.

Now please, please don't sit there and act like you all didn't have the plastic floor runners all over your house too. You know you had the plastic floor runners in the living room and going up and down the steps.

And all for what?

To preserve and protect your valuables from being damaged.

When we look at the following scriptures, you can get an idea of what I mean.

Scripture Reading:
Psalms 55:22 reads, *"Cast thy burden upon the Lord, and He shall sustain thee: He shall never suffer the righteous to be moved."* **-KJV**
1Cor. 6:20 reads, *"For ye are bought with a price: therefore, glorify God in your body, and in your spirit, which are God's."* - **KJV**

You see just like my mom, who used plastic to cover her valuables and to protect her investments, the Almighty God did the very same thing for us. Though we were never perfect before, during and after the process, God still saw fit to cover us with His Blood.

Not only did Jesus' death cover our sins on the cross, but His Blood which was used to protect us from the sins we committed on yesterday; is that same unchangeable, never ending, everlasting Blood that protects and covers us today and will continue to redeem us on tomorrow and forever more. Which now brings us to a place called deliverance. And the question that comes to mind is, what is deliverance?

What is deliverance?

According to The Concordance Bible Dictionary, the word **deliverance** is defined as *having* *liberation; to be redeemed. Deliverance means to be discharged, to be rescued; to be set free.*

And I know God never does this, but you see when I get paid every two weeks, the first thing I do is pay my tithes electronically. I send it straight from my checking account to the church's account. And I know I shouldn't feel like it's a burden, but to me it is. I feel like I have to pay my tithes because I know how much I owe God.

I know God will never hold a bounty or a price over my head and I know the Lord won't ever make me feel like "you remember when I woke you up this morning" right, so I just don't ever forget to pay my tithes.

Yes, I know, I shouldn't place that kind of weight on myself, but I can't help it. I owe God everything. I know God doesn't operate like that, but I know what I owe Him. He's done so much for me. And I can't begin to tell it all. I can't begin to thank Him for all the Victories. I can't begin to thank Him for all the mess He's seen me through.

I said all that to say this; I feel free when I pay my tithes. God gave me the strength and the capability to get up and go to work every day. Well first, He gave me a job, right, so all these things and more, I have to make it to show God how much I appreciate Him. And one way in doing so, is by paying my tithes.

Watch this, we all have been subject to, bound, emotionally, physically, mentally, financially and yes even spiritually handcuff to something and or someone, who has or have made it their sole purpose to **try** and taint what is considered valuable.
And a thought of some kind has been planted in our minds to make us sometimes feel like because we have been violated and or taken advantage of in one way or another; that we are no longer seen as valuable.

Can I share something with you right here?

The devil is a LIAR!!

I'm here to encourage you, that when the Lord Jesus Christ lent you and I to our parents. And birth us into this world, we were already redeemed as valuable to and through the word of God.
Yes, we were born in sin, but God wipe the slate clean, Praise the Lord.

Scripture Reading:
Psalms 139:14 reads, *I will praise thee; I am fearfully and wonderfully made: marvelous are thy works; and that my soul knoweth right well.* - **KJV**

Beloved, we are valuable to God and to the body of Christ. Why? God took the time to place His Spiritual

DNA (The Holy Ghost) and strategically in beaded that irresistible source down on the inside of every one of us the children of God.

When we begin to feel lost, abandon or unappreciated even, it is that spiritual DNA that provides a reassurance that we belong, not to the world, but to the Creator of this world.

When this world tries to weigh us down with its lies, deception, burdens, conflicts, tricks, witchcraft, dark magic and negative energy it is the word of God that has been planted down on the inside of us that has, will and continue to bring us encouragement. It is the DNA of our Powerful God that will shield us from the forces of darkness. It is that God given love that sustains us from the negative pollution of life.

When Jesus died on the cross for you and for me, we were set free from the things that were meant to hold us bondage. Those very things that the world knew would try to subject us to its will are the very things Christ sacrificed His life for. That makes us Valuable.

Yes, we are tried, persecuted and envied, but that's only because we have something that this world can't have, and this world can't take away, the Holy Ghost.

And even though we fall short of God's word sometimes, even though we did and do things that wasn't and isn't pleasing to God and we found our mistakes to be embarrassing, Hallelujah, God says, I still see your value. I still see your freedom.

Scripture Reading:
Leviticus 26:13 - *KJV* reads, *I am the Lord your God, which brought you forth out of the land of Egypt, that ye should not be their bondmen; and I have broken the bands of your yoke, and made you go upright.*

God is sharing with us how to fight and hold on to our freedom. Listen, why do you think God designed it so, that we die daily (repent)?

God gave us the gift of repentance so that we would not have to walk around, hunched over carrying heavy luggage filled with all of our sins and mistakes.

Please don't take this the wrong way when I say this, but it's not God's fault that you are carrying this load. God has already forgiving you (through repentance), now it's up to you to forgive yourself. And once you and I have made up in our minds to forgive ourselves, then that will start the healing process of having a peace of mind.

Alright, so the question is; what does it mean in Having a Peace of Mind?

Having a Peace of Mind can be better understood as: Having to support; to keep or to nurture your freedom.

Note: Here are some scriptures that I want us read to cover us while maintaining our Deliverance.

Scripture Reading:

Psalms 46:10 NLT - *'"Be still, and know that I am God! I will be honored by every nation. I will be honored throughout the world."'*

Psalms 71:1 NLT - *'O Lord, I have come to you for protection; don't let me be disgraced.'*

John 8:34-36 NLT - *'v34 Jesus replied, "I tell you the truth, everyone who sins is a slave of sin.*

'v35 A slave is not a permanent member of the family, but a son is part of the family forever.

'v36 So if the Son sets you free, you are truly free. '

1Cor. 2:16 NLT - *'For, "Who can know the Lord 's thoughts? Who knows enough to teach him?" But we understand these things, for we have the mind of Christ.'*

11 Cor. 3:17 NLT - *'For the Lord is the Spirit, and wherever the Spirit of the Lord is, there is freedom. '*

With that being said:
Turn to Philippians the 4th chapter and let's look at verse 7.

Phil. 4:7 ***NLT -*** *'And now, dear brothers and sisters, one final thing. Fix your thoughts on what is true, and* *honorable, and right, and pure, and lovely, and admirable. Think about things that are excellent and worthy of praise. '*

The book of Philippians was written by Paul. And when Paul wrote this book to the believers, he wanted to leave the believers instructions in Christian Unity, so he shared with them to not focus on the worries and the stresses of life, but to focus more on their prayer life.

2
Having a Peace of Mind
A Strong Prayer Life

February 6, 2020

To have a peace of mind, there are several essential things that are needed to help develop that character. The first thing you will need is to have a strong prayer life.

Well, what is prayer?

Prayer my sisters and brothers, is that divine connection from our hearts to God's ear. When you pray, you are having an intimate conversation with the one you love the most.

Someone you can talk to in-private or in-person. You don't care about who maybe watching you, you don't care about who maybe listening to you. All you know is, you're in the presence of your Lover. You just know that you are talking to the only one that understands you better than anyone else ever could, Amen.

Follow me on this, talking to God doesn't take all the, "Thou Art the sun maker, the one who calm the raging seas. Thou art the king of….

Scripture Reading:
1 Samuel 1:9-18 ref verses 10, 11 & 12 ***NLT*** – *10 Hannah was in deep anguish, crying bitterly as she prayed to the Lord. 11 And she made a vow: "O Lord of Heaven's Armies, if you will look upon my sorrow and answer my prayer and give me a son, then I will give him back to you. He will be yours for his entire lifetime, and as a sign that he has been dedicated to the Lord, his*

hair will never be cut." 12 As she was praying to the Lord, Eli watched her.

When Hannah prayed to the Lord about her concerns, not one time did she care about who was watching and or listening. The only thing she knew was I gotta talk to the Master.

Yes, her heart was heavy and rightfully so, but Hannah also knew that the only way she could get her burdens lifted, she needed to go to God in prayer. She couldn't wait until she got back home to possibly get in her secret closet. She needed a word from God right here and now.

That sounds just like us doesn't it?

Whenever life is trying to get the very best of us, we don't have time to waste. We need to hear from God right now. And even though sometimes it may seem like God isn't listening or not there. Trust me Beloved God is always listening to hear the voice of His OWN. Despite what others may say, regardless of the situation; God is behind the scenes working things out for our good.

Look, God just wants you to talk to Him about every and anything. Now even though God already knows, still He wants you to have an open relationship with Him. And watch this, God is so smart, wise and knowledgeable, and I mean God knows absolutely everything that there is to know about us, and that's what you call ***omniscient.***

According to Merriam-Webster the word ***Omniscient*** is defined as – *"All-knowing, All-wise and All-seeing God."*

God saw the issues, the problems, the let downs, disappointments, the Victory's, the healings, the delivery's, the careers, the promotions, the lies we told, the lies told on us, I mean God knows and seen them all, but He just wants us to come to Him in prayer to talk about all these things, though He knows all things.

And let me put a clip note here, God doesn't hold grudges, we do not serve a God like that. Once we made it right with Him, it is God that forgives. Watch this, now the reason we can't grow or move forward is because we have yet to forgive ourselves of the mistake(s) we caused. And God tells us in His word in Matt 18:21 to stop counting the losses and consider the potential wins. And not just in our lives, but also in the lives of others.

Scripture Reading:
Matthew 18:21-22 *NLT* - *'v21 Then Peter came to him and asked, "Lord, how often should I forgive someone who sins against me? Seven times?" v22 "No, not seven times," Jesus replied, "but seventy times seven!*

Here is Peter asking Jesus a question in a form of a prayer. And Jesus' reply was, "No, not seven times, but seventy times seven." So, if Jesus is telling Peter to forgive someone for whatever he has done, then we ought to forgive ourselves as well as others.

And though at times it may seem hard or a bit taxing to forgive someone for the same or different offenses, we are still obligated to forgive them. We are obligated to show them mercy. I mean truthfully speaking, how many times will God show us mercy for our wrong doings if we do not show leniency to others?

I just wanted to put that footnote there just in case someone is fighting against themselves. Hallelujah, I'm encouraging you beloved to stop fighting yourself and let it go.

Ok, let's turn Isaiah 65:24 And we are going to be reading from both the King James and the New Living Translations. KJV *And it shall come to pass*, (now let's look at this, look at this 1st line. And it shall come to pass. Jesus is already saying that it's over, but we are still crying and worrying about things the Lord has or will soon deliver us from it and or through it. And I'm not saying this to be mean, but my Sisters and Brothers, it's time to get over it, it's over. Alright?)

And it shall come to pass, that before they call, I will answer. (You see, that's goes back to the omniscient God. The God that knows everything. I already know what you are going through. I was there while you were in it and I'll be there when you come out of it, but I still want you to talk to me, why because, I want to have a relationship with you. Jesus is saying just because I know, your wants, needs and desires doesn't mean that we can't talk.) Let's read some more, *while they are yet speaking, I will hear.*

If we want Jesus to hear us, we've got to build a strong prayer life and build a strong relationship with Him. The Lord Jesus Christ is giving us time to build with Him. And it would so discouraging to see that we had time and didn't make the time, if or when those unchilling words would come from the Master, depart from me, for I know you not. We don't ever want to be placed in a position when God says, "Do I know you?"

Let's take a look at that real quick, turn to Matthew 7:21-23.

Matthew 7:21-23 ***NLT*** **- '21** *"Not everyone who calls out to me, 'Lord! Lord!' will enter the Kingdom of Heaven. Only those who actually do the will of my Father in heaven will enter.* **22** *On judgment day many will say to me, 'Lord! Lord! We prophesied in your name and cast out demons in your name and performed many miracles in your name.'* **23** *But I will reply, 'I never knew you. Get away from me, you who break God's laws."*

Here in these verses, Jesus is telling the disciples to handle their business better than what they are doing. If you continue to know what to do as a child of the

King and you continue to not follow my instructions for your life, then I will have to deny you, like you are denying me.

Please Lord Jesus.

That's sounds like a real relationship doesn't it?

Well, if you aren't speaking, I'm not speaking. How in the name are we going to win with that kind of temperament?

We can't afford to not remain in someone's good grace or vice versa, why, because we are in a relationship. And the only difference between you, me, us and Christ is, Jesus has nothing to lose, but we have everything to lose, even, our lives.

Alright, let's go back a bit before verses 21-23 to Matthew 7:7-11

Scripture Reading:
Matthew 7: 7-11 *NLT* – it reads, 7 *"Keep on asking,*
and you will receive what you ask for. Keep on seeking,
and you will find. Keep on knocking, and the door will
be opened to you. '**8** *For everyone who asks, receives.*
Everyone who seeks, finds. And to everyone who knocks,
the door will be opened. **9** *"You parents—if your*
children ask for a loaf of bread, do you give them a

stone instead? **10** *Or if they ask for a fish, do you give them a snake?*
Of course not! **11** *So if you sinful people know how to give good gifts to your children, how much more will your heavenly Father give good gifts to those who ask him.'*

In having a strong prayer life, your prayers have to be effective. Your prayers have to get the attention of God. If you want to see God move on your behalf, you have to pray the prayer of a Victor and not a victim. (well Lord I done all I know how to do, I might as well… Listen we serve a Mighty God. And God doesn't have time for a weak or unemotional or a motionless prayer language. God needs to hear prayers from those who are ready to receive the blessings.

You're unemployed, but your prayer language is, "God I thank you for this new career change."

Your living situation is not the best. The landlord keeps increasing the rent and won't do anything about the bugs. Your prayer language should be, "Lord, I thank you for my new house where I am the landlord and I am bug free."

You checked for a deposit and the money is gone. You asked your husband, "what happened to the money?" His response is," Oh, me and the fellas are hanging out tonight." Your prayer language should be, Lord, thank you for delivering my husband from spending all the money and thank you for delivering him from the street life."

You know that you have good children, right?

Sure, you do. And you want to see them have the best in life. You try to warn them about the darkness of this world, and they think they know it all, been everywhere and know everybody. And then they get introduced to something that they can't turn a loose and now they've become a slave to it. And while you are yet covering them with the Blood of Jesus, your prayer language should be, "Lord, I want to thank you for delivering my child(ren) from this.

The truth of the matter is this, we all deserve to be loved and want to be loved, even if you have fooled yourself to think that you don't; you do. And there is no Greater Love that I rather have than the love of Jesus Christ.

3
Having a Peace of Mind
Confession is Good for the Soul

February 13, 2020

Now, I know some of us may have a concern with the word confession, but there is nothing about this word that should sway us one way or the other; unless we do not understand what the word confession truly means.

So, let's jump right in.

According to the world dictionary, the word ***confession*** means: '*something that is confessed; a formal, usually written, acknowledgment of guilt by a person accused of a crime.'*

So, let's go back a little bit. Confession is something that is confessed.
Confess or confessed is to be charged or to be made guilty; in other words, to own a guilt or a fault.

Now according to *The New Combined Bible Dictionary and Concordance*; Confession is defined as '*admission of a wrong or to an agreement with a fact.'*

I know, I know you have this weird look on your face right now, don't you, like Pastor what does that mean?

Well, did you see what just happened here between man's variation and God's definition in dealing with the word confession?
Man's definition of confession means to lock us into something that we can't ever get ourselves out of.

Where God's definition of confession leads us in a direction of getting out of or yet having a way out of something. And that way is through repentance.

What is Repentance?

According to Eerdmans Dictionary of the Bible, the Greek word for ***Repentance*** is *metanoeo* which means to understand something differently after thinking it over.

When we have reevaluated our mistakes and come to the conclusion that a change in us is so desperately needed. We are soon convicted or strongly convinced to repent for our errors to God so that He can wipe the slate clean, not *with* man, but ***through*** Christ.

Well, Pastor what is the difference between Confession and Repentance?
Confession is admission or admitting to something, Repentance is remission (means to be forgiven) from something.
Confession says you are going pay for what you did, all while Repentance says your debt was already paid.

Lord Have Mercy!!

Scripture Reading:
Alright, real quick turn to **Daniel 9:4** ***NLT*** – '*v***4**
"I prayed to the Lord my God and confessed:
"O Lord, you are a great and awesome God! You always fulfill your covenant and keep your promises of unfailing love to those who love you and obey your commands.
'**5** *But we have sinned and done wrong. We have rebelled against you and scorned your commands and regulations.*

Now, did you see what Daniel just did? In verse 4, Daniel started off by acknowledging God for who He was to him in his life. He then confessed for his own sins to God, but by the time he got to verse 5, he started repenting for everyone else's sins too. Look at verse 5, *but We have sinned and done wrong.*

Daniel didn't point the finger on who did what. He didn't do like Adam and Eve in the garden of Eden when God asked Adam why did you do it? And Adam and Eve, played the blaming game. She made me do it, no, the snake made me do it.

Daniel said these are my people and I don't want to see them go to hell, so let me go to God on their behalf. And hopefully they are doing the same for me. But if not it's ok, because I already went to God about everything, for everything.

You see confession is not just for you. Confession is for anyone and everyone who are divinely attached and or connected to you. So, when we are pointing the figure at someone else's mistakes, God is saying what are you doing to encourage, to help, to mentor, or even cover that person in prayer, so that they too can be forgiven. Confession and Repentance have to work on all areas of life, Amen.

Let's take a look at **James 5:16** ***NLT*** **– '*v*16**
Confess your sins to each other and pray for each other

so that you maybe healed. The earnest prayer of a righteous person has great power and produces wonderful results.

Ok, what James is saying here is, when we confess our sins to one another and pray for each other. We are made whole and or healed...

Watch this, when I pray for you and you pray for me; we are or should be asking God to forgive you, me, us of the sins, it is then that God heals and frees us from that sin. Not so that we can go back or to keep sinning, but to redeem us from any charges that maybe held against you.

Now let me say this, please Beloved, be very careful who or to whom you confess to. There are some people (inside and outside of your circle) that has been statically placed all around us with Satan's troops who are just waiting to tell ALL of your business. And before you hang up the phone, they're already dialing the gossiping network station, running down every intimate part of who you are to someone else. It then becomes a domino effect where that person told someone, they tell someone and that someone went and told someone else. Causing you to look foolish in the eyes of others

And it is terrifyingly strange to me how people you thought you could trust start gossiping about you, when all along their closets are bursting at the seams with their past regrets. Yet they are hoping, begging and pleading with God to don't ever let their sins out of the closet.

If we would spend more time cleaning up our own act (examining ourselves) and leaving everybody else's life alone we would be in a far better state of mind, but some of us have the, "I gotta know disease."

That's why I encourage you to be sure to ask God to increase or to enhance your gift of discernment. Believe it or not, we all have the gift of discernment. We just have to tap into it and exercise it and make it worthwhile to us.

And just for clarity, Discernment or the gift to discern is allowing the Holy Spirit to announce to you if this person or that person is genuine. And yes, sometimes we don't always get it right. We think because this person has this background that they are no good when they are the complete opposite. In other words, don't judge a person's appearance, but study or take a good look at their heart.

Now at the same time, as I am praying for you and you should be praying for me. And here we need to be careful, because when a sister or brother comes to us in secret, and ask us to pray, it is our duty as a Believer and Lover of God's word that we honor that request. Why, look at the later part of verse of James 5:16. It is the effectual *(Powerful)* fervent *(burning or glow)* prayer

of the righteous man that availeth *(the eth means never ending; on-going)* much.
The later of verse 16 reads, *The earnest prayer of a righteous person has great power and produces wonderful results.*

You see, the word earnest means to pledge or to promise. If you are in need of prayer, you have to go find someone who will make a promise to cover you in prayer and tarry right there with you. And the word tarry means to wait or to hold out. When you find someone, who is willing to take an oath to speak over your life. And while they are speaking, they are waiting right there with you to see the prophetic change that will soon impregnate your Spirit.

Man, Oh Man

Scripture Reading:
1John 1:8-9 ***NLT*** – '8 *If we claim we have no sin, we are only fooling ourselves and not living in the truth.*
'9 *But if we confess our sins to Him, He is faithful and just to forgive us our sins and to cleanse us from all wickedness.*

Not me, but if we confess our sins to God, the word of God states that God is faithful and just to not only forgive our sins, Hallelujah, but He will also cleanse us from not just 1st, 2nd, 3rd, 100th, but all wickedness.

You see God wants us to know, remember and understand that we are His Ambassadors. We are His Chosen vessels to do and complete a Mighty work that's been assigned to us. We are to constantly encourage those who are facing similar issues that we not too long ago have been delivered from. And no, it doesn't have to be anything what you've been through exactly, but in order to be a witness, we have got to have gone through something in order to tell someone else how God saw us through it.

And everyone we come in contact with, you really don't have to say a word, why because it's your light that shines so bright, that people are going to want to know how did you make it, how did you survive it? And without wavering, you can honestly tell them that it was nobody but Jesus.

I remember a few Sunday's ago, I preached about a young lady who was actually named Sin because of her past. But she found that Jesus was in town and went looking for Him to confess her sins. And this young lady repented without saying word. She was so remorseful, that she fell on top of Jesus's feet, cried so hard that she drenched the Master's feet with her tears, then dried His feet with her hair. And while all this was going on, people were still holding on to her past, remembering on who she was, but Jesus was and still is remembering on who you are, not who you were.

God Help!!

Isn't weird, how you want to grow up, move on, get healed, get delivered and be set free. And no matter how much you try, there is always somebody hanging around trying to get you to remember who you use to be. You have every right to tell them, that God sees you for who you are and not who you were.

You have every right to tell them that you are a child of the King!!!

4 Having a Peace of Mind Forgiveness is Crucial

February 20, 2020

In our previous, as well as our next few series of, "Having a Peace of Mind" it will be important to us to gravitate solely to what the Bible is sharing with us, why, because we will all be tested to make sure that we truly understand what it means to be freed or better yet to be delivered in a sense of having a peace of mind.

And what that means is that every sub-topic that we embrace under this heading, "Having A Peace of Mind" will strengthen us and redefine us to a place where the very things that are around us will not cause us to act nor react unseemly.

But in fact, cause us to rise above it.

Hallelujah, so let's dig into this word forgiveness.

- Forgive or forgiveness is a prerequisite; it is a requirement that the children of God must exercise on a daily basis, why because in order for us maintain the Full Grace of God, in order for us to maintain the Full Favor of God, Hallelujah, we have to, we must extend Forgiveness to everybody.

So, the question that one maybe thinking; what is forgiveness?

According to "The New Combined Bible Dictionary and Concordance," written by Charles F. Pheiffer, Forgiveness is defined as one who is pardon of a fault.

Many times, in life as we have seen it, people all around us even ourselves have managed to do something that needed forgiving from.

Regardless if it were by accident or by act of deviousness, that fault needed forgiveness. When we ponder over an incident for a period of time, our hearts would have become harden so much so that we tend to take out the frustration on someone else.

And when an innocent bystander, who has become a victim of your past. When your sister and or your brother has done nothing more but try to sympathize with your hurt, grief, pain, neglect. They are only there for moral support, but your previous encounter has become so abrasive that no one wants to deal with you

Are you with me?

And after the Holy Ghost has convicted you. And you realize the mess you've made. You are now left at the mercy of someone else to forgive your fault. Ahhh God
Leaving you to plead for the one you've offended for grace.

And grace is a pardon that we do not deserve.

Well, isn't that what God gives us, Grace?

Here's a mental note: *Our Salvation from sin is not based on our forgiving others.*
Salvation is given simply because that's the will of God. but we can't receive God's forgiveness until we realize what forgiveness really means so that we can apply forgiveness to those who has done wrong by us. Praise the Lord

If you have your Bibles, turn to **Matthew 6:14-15 NLT**...read "**12** *and forgive us our sins, as we have forgiven those who sin against us.* **13** *And don't let us yield to temptation, but rescue us from the evil one.* **14** *If* *you forgive those who sin against you, your heavenly Father will forgive you.* **15** *But if you refuse to forgive others, your Father will not forgive your sins."*

Through this prayer, Jesus gives the disciples as well as you and I a lesson in the blessings of forgiving others and warnings when we don't forgive. Christ is constantly reminding us that in order to retain the kingdom of God; we must live a life like Christ. And in living a life like Christ, we 1st must have a relationship with Christ.

Here in the book of Matthew, chapter 6, Jesus was teaching on giving to the needy. Now moving throughout the scriptures starting with verses 5 through 18, the disciples were concerned about their prayer life, so they asked the Master Teacher to teach them to pray. Keep in mind one of the key components in order to have a peace of mind, we've got to stay in constant communion with the Lord.

What does that entitle?

When we are constantly having communion with our Lord and Saviour Jesus Christ, and communion here means to be connected. We have to share with the Lord everything that's going on with us. I mean after all; it was Christ who made us right?

So, if Christ made us, why should we tell Him if He already knows?

Christ knows our heart Yes, 1000 times Yes, but keep in mind, we are the voice for the Lord. So, when we share with the Lord on what's going on with us; In other words, when we go to God in prayer, for everything about everything, we are speaking in the atmosphere on what's going on with us, what we are in need of from the Master.

Just as the same, the Lord knows about our desires.

When we tell the Lord about the dreams and desires. And keep in mind that it is the Lord who plants those dreams and desires into our thought process to begin with.

And He just wants us to confirm with Him what He already knows, God Help us!!!

So, I just wanted to place that footnote there, but let's take a look at verse 14.

14 *If you forgive those who sin against you, your heavenly Father will forgive you.*

Well, what did we just define forgiveness as? To Excuse and or to Pardon; To let an incident go. We are going to be tested on Having A Peace of Mind. And how do we keep that Spirit of Peace?

By separating ourselves from those things that are not meant to be in our space. In other words, let it go.

And I get it, sometimes we want to hold to a grievance, to the disappointment, sometimes to the embarrassment, because of the situation. Listen, when we have a relationship with God, and His Spirit growing down on the inside of us, there is nothing that we cannot handle. Why?

Because Greater is He that is in me than he of the world.

Look at verse 15.
15 *But if you refuse to forgive others, your Father will not forgive your sins."*

Ok well we just talked about this, go back to what we just wrote down....
In order for us to receive the forgiveness of God, we've got to learn to let things go. Any and everything that is not of God's will for us we must get rid of it. We are instructed through the word of God to let it go.

Jump up to verse 12
12 *and forgive us our sins, as we have forgiven those who sin against us*

We must be careful when dealing with this verse and what proceeds, because we have just God to forgive us of our mess, but we dropped the ball when forgiving our brother and or sister of their mistakes.

The word Forgive is a verb, and it shows double action.

According to the Bible Dictionary and Concordance, the word Forgive is defined as *to be excused or to be pardon from.*

Watch this, the word forgive is a 2-syllable word. The *For* (F.O.R) in forgive is defined as in order to obtain or to gain. The word *give* is defined as to offer without expectation. So, when we forgive someone of a fault, mistake, an error or whatever you want to name it; we are actually placing that pardon into effect.

In other words, when we forgive, we forgive someone for whatever the reason. We are offering them something without any expectations, why because our Heavenly Father will set the order and He will make sure we gain. God will make sure that we get it all back. I tell you it's a double action when it comes to forgiveness.

HAVING A PEACE OF MIND
FORGIVENESS IS CRUCIAL PART 2

March 12, 2020
We are still under the sub-topic: Forgiveness is crucial.

Sometime ago during our discussions, I asked you all to write down a few scriptures that will help us along the way of forgiving others. These verses as you know have the complete saving power to bring us out of darkness, hallelujah as well as render our enemies powerless.

And sometimes it seems like you can't escape the clutches of your oppressor no doubt because you work with, go to school with, go to church with, even go to bed with. And Trust me, I totally understand that sometimes you would rather ignore or forget that the incident ever happened, but God is requiring in order for us to grow in grace you and I, the Children of God be an example and be that bright beam of light for others to see that just like the flu, forgiving others can spread all across this nation causing people to be filled with the Holy Ghost. Causing people to be set free.

You know and they know they have done you wrong. They want to say good morning, or better yet I'm sorry, but they're afraid, afraid that you will reject them or even worst, refuse to forgive them.

Lord Have Mercy!!

You say you have forgiven them, but you really haven't, because if you had,
1.) it wouldn't be eating you up so bad, meaning you wouldn't keep thinking or talking about it to others. Your jaws wouldn't get tight when you see them
2.) Those who have done you wrong wouldn't feel so weighed down by it. You have got to let that thing go before it stain the very relationship you are trying so hard to build with the Lord.

God Help!!

Scripture Reading:
Ephesians 4:26-29 - '**26** *And "don't sin by letting anger control you." Don't let the sun go down while you are still angry, '*

It's ok to be upset, but do not act nor react on it. You can be angry, but don't try to do them dirty, because they threw you under the bus.

Let not the sun go down upon your wrath. My Sisters and Brothers, I know you are waiting for God to fix it, but God has already given you the power to fix the problem. (Let It Go!!! Hallelujah, Let It Go, Forgive Them and Let It Go!!!)

'**27** *for anger gives a foothold to the devil.'*

Neither give place to the devil. Under no circumstances are we to give in to what the devil wants. (To see us fail, to see us make a fool out of ourselves.) Don't give in to the *I'm going to get you back* syndrome, because once you fall into that trap, it will be very hard for you to get out of it.
And I'm not saying that God can't free us from it, He absolutely can, but we didn't free Johnny from his wrong, we didn't free Donna from her mistake, so why should God free us from ours??

'v28 And "don't sin by letting anger control you." Don't let the sun go down while you are still angry, for anger gives a foothold to the devil. If you are a thief, quit stealing. Instead, use your hands for good hard work, and then give generously to others in need. '

Listen, we have got to make a plan of action to be healed and instead of being destroyed. And what I mean by destroyed, I mean the very fabrication of a person's thoughts can cause them to make a mistake. Causing them to look foolish due to their actions.

So, Pastor are you saying that in order for me to be freed or in order for me to be forgiven I have to forgive that person who's done me wrong?

That's exactly what I am saying. No matter what they have done, we've got to forgive them.

Listen, I am a living testimony of what I am sharing with you. I had a family member who tried to bring my name to shame, and I was Mad as fire for a while at that person. I knew I had to forgive him or her in order for God to move bountifully in my life, my marriage and my Calling.

In my mind I was thinking of ways to get them back for what they tried to do, but I knew in my spirit that if I went after them, God would come after me. I didn't speak to that person for months. I hated them for their jealous actions, but deep in my heart, I knew I had to get it off me before I turned bitter.

We would be hypocrites if we think that God should free us from our mistakes and refuse to free others of their wrong.

We would be fooling ourselves if we want the full blessing of God but refuse to put in the work to receive the blessing of God.

Watch This!! When we, the children of God allow the Holy Spirit to lead, guide, and give us direction. We are waiving our rights to work on our own merit. In a fair exchange, we have made the ultimate choice to constantly work on the characteristics that will render us qualified for Having a peace of mind.

So, what makes us qualified Pastor?

There is a two-fold transaction that needs to take place in order for God's people to be free.

For the first part, turn to Luke 23:46 ***KJV*** – *And when Jesus cried out with a loud voice, he said, Father, into thy hands I commend my spirit: and having said thus, he gave up the ghost.*

Now According to The New Combined Bible Dictionary by Charles F. Pfeiffer.

The word **commend** means to deliver with confidence.

Now to me, the word commend means - to willingly give back to the Original Giver for safe keeping.

Now there are 3 people who are involved here. And these three brothers had dialogue in reference to verse 46. They had a conversation on how to handle the situations that came, that is here and that will come.

These three Brothers call themselves, "The Trinity." And the Trinity knew that this world would not be able to survive on its own and would constantly be harassed by the sins of this world if something were not done to free her of it.

Now before we move forward, I want to make sure that we are all on the same page when I said, "The Trinity." The Trinity consists of three people: God the Father, God the Son and God the Holy Ghost.

We are made free through Jesus Christ who by releasing of the Holy Ghost and sending his spirit back to His Father, Almighty God.

The second part to this phase, turn to **Galatians 5: 1, 13, 16-26** ....

Galatians 5:1 ***NLT*** – *So Christ has truly set us free. Now make sure that you stay free, and don't get tied up again in slavery to the law.*

Paul, the writer of the book Galatians has warned the city of Galatia and is warning us right now to don't get caught up, don't be so easily swayed or tricked, don't allow anything or anyone to cause you to fall under the law of slavery, which is sin.

Galatians 5:13 ***NLT*** – *For you have been called to live in freedom, my brothers and sisters. But don't use your* *freedom to satisfy your sinful nature. Instead, use your freedom to serve one another in love.*

March 19, 2020

So, on last week, we talked about There being a two-fold transaction or a two-part deal that needs to take place in order for God's people to be free.

The first part was when we turn to Luke 23:46 ***KJV*** – *And when Jesus cried out with a loud voice, he said, Father, into thy hands I commend my spirit: and having said thus, he gave up the ghost.*

Commend- Now According to The New Combined Bible Dictionary by Charles F. Pfeiffer.

And the second phase for God's people being free, we left off in the book of Galatians the 5th chapter and starting at verse 1

Gaining the full access to God's Glory, which is the peace of God, we the children of God must share the work in keeping or staying clear of those things that want to destroy our character. We have been handpicked by God Himself to do great things on the earth and the enemy knows this.

Listen, anytime you've made up in your right mind to follow the will of God, the enemy is always there lurking, trying to see how he can alter and manipulate the plan of God.

Hallelujah, but what the enemy continues to not understand is this, that when you are consistent in being or becoming an annoyance, God will make the ultimate decision in dealing with you. That's why the Bible declares in **Isaiah 41:10- NKJ** *"Fear not, for I am with you; Be not dismayed, for I am your God. I will strengthen you, yes, I will help you, I will uphold you with My righteous right hand.*

Now watch this, the **NLT** reads this way. *"Don't be afraid, for I am with you. Don't be discouraged, for I am your God. I will strengthen you and help you. I will hold you up with my victorious right hand."*

God my Spirit is happy.

Listen, when we fall into deep waters, it is not to punish us or to press us down. It is to show that God has All Power. When our backs are against the wall and we are ready to give in to whatever. God reminds in His word that He will hold us up and with His Powerful and Victorious right hand, God says we still win. Why, because it is the peace of God that reminds us that we belong to Him.

And see he (the enemy), will try to place any form of a stumbling block in our way, but I plead the blood of Jesus on every trap that the enemy try to set.

And God is so powerful and so smart that He will allow the enemy access in your space. And grant the enemy some room to plant a seed of doubt, fear or whatever just to get us to think the negative; when all along that little seed that was trying to give birth was actually used by God to get us to pray harder. Causing us to succeed, God get the Glory and the enemy gets back under the heel of our feet.

Scripture Reading:
Let's take a look at **Galatians 5:16-26 NLT** – ***v16*** *'So I say, let the Holy Spirit guide your lives. Then you won't be doing what your sinful nature craves.*

This word is telling us that when we allow the Holy Ghost to give us direction in every situation of life, we the children of God will always have the peace of God, which means we have a peace of Mind. Amen, we don't have the time nor the energy in remembering what we did last year, last month, last night or even 5 minutes ago.
The peace of God comes in when we ask God the Father to forgive our past, right?

And in doing so God honors the request, but we get so pickled down with what took place in our past that we start thinking God is not going to forgive me this one. I really messed this one up. I don't see how God will let this one go.

And my question to you is, who told you that?

When God clearly told you in **Isaiah 41:10** *"I am your God (I know the challenges you are having), He said, ... I will give you strength."*

There is no way in the world I would bring you out of one thing and allow you to suffer alone in another. Hallelujah

*'**v17** The sinful nature wants to do evil, which is just the opposite of what the Spirit wants. And the Spirit gives us desires that are the opposite of what the sinful nature desires. These two forces are constantly fighting each other, so you are not free to carry out your good intentions.*

You notice when we give new year resolutions, and we say I'm going to do this; I'm going to do that. This year I am determined to lose 25 lbs., but as soon as we make that statement, here's where the temptation or the sinful nature starts to pop up. You see a commercial of your favorite ice cream, now all of a sudden, your mind is haunting you to go to get the ice cream.

And God is saying to us that if we want to win this battle against that sinful nature, we've got to do our part which is to believe that God has already fixed this thing for us.

Now here's a cross reference turn to **Exodus 14:14-** *The Lord himself will fight for you. Just stay calm.* **NLT**

God has already promised to fight our battles. And sometimes our battles come from within. And trying to fight all forms of addictions can be taxing enough...

Scripture Reading:

Galatians 5:18-26 NLT ***'v18*** *But when you are directed by the Spirit, you are not under obligation to the law of Moses.*
'v19 *When you follow the desires of your sinful nature, the results are very clear: sexual immorality, impurity, lustful pleasures,*
'v20 *idolatry, sorcery, hostility, quarreling, jealousy, outbursts of anger, selfish ambition, dissension, division,*
'v21 *envy, drunkenness, wild parties, and other sins like these. Let me tell you again, as I have before, that anyone living that sort of life will not inherit the Kingdom of God.*
'v22 *But the Holy Spirit produces this kind of fruit in our lives: love, joy, peace, patience, kindness, goodness, faithfulness,*
'v23 *gentleness, and self-control. There is no law against these things!*
'v24 *Those who belong to Christ Jesus have nailed the passions and desires of their sinful nature to his cross and crucified them there.*
'v25 *Since we are living by the Spirit, let us follow the Spirit's leading in every part of our lives.*
'v26 *Let us not become conceited, or provoke one another, or be jealous of one another.'*

5
Having a Peace of Mind
Trust God, No Matter What

March 26, 2020

In all our endeavors of life's ups and downs, planned and unplanned, our good days, our bad days it is quite evident that the one person we can always lean and depend on, that we can always trust, is Jesus. For some time now, I have been in constant prayer that God will be quick to heal this nation.

However, I am just wandering, in order to get this world back on the right track I'm wondering if God has allowed this plague to overthrow things so that folks can get back to depending, leaning and trusting in God, Hallelujah.

As we watch the news and social media, we see Police Officers literally using the powers granted by the state to commit random shootings as well as falsely accusing and or making unlegalized arrests. Not caring that they are being recorded or not, they are just on a blood thirsty hunt to kill what they feel to be a threat.

It's been said that young men from ages 16-35 are shooting and killing each other for little to no reason at all. And over what, money, drugs and or girls. And now they have become so bold to commit these meaningless crimes in the broad daylight. They don't care about who's watching them, and they wish someone would say something to them to give them a just cause to say or do something to you.

Here recently the state of Maryland like other surrounding states has become a playground for sex trafficking children. It's been displayed all over the news and Social Media that Government Officials are found sitting in strip clubs while on duty; instead of protecting our Cities, Communities, and our Women and Children from such a disgrace. I'm telling you, now is the time more than ever that we need to trust God.

And these things along with countless others has brought us to place of seeking God more now than ever when embracing Having A Peace of Mind. And in doing so like Israel, the world is now forced into a place of understanding on how to Trust God through No Matter What.

What is Trust?

According to," The World Dictionary," **trust** is defined as - confident expectation of something; hope.

According to, "The New Combined Bible Dictionary," **trust** is defined as – A reliance or resting of the mind on the integrity, justice or friendship of another person.

In other words, trust means to believe in or depend on something and or on someone else.

Psalms 118:8 – NLT - *It is better to take refuge in the Lord than to trust in people.*

Many of us find it hard or challenging turning that much power over to someone else. Relying on the fact that someone will do what they say they will do. We've went through so many changes and obstacles believing someone would come through for us, right? When all along we were setup to be let down. And life changing events and experiences has taught us never to put that much trust in a person or people ever again.

And God is saying to us, I know what man has done to you and I didn't come to challenge your trust, but rather I come to infuse that trust.
God says, I admit, man can be a bit messy at times, but that's why I sent my Son, Jesus Christ, Amen, so that through Him, I could fix the mess man has made.

Let's look at **II Samuel 22:31- KJV-** *'As for God, his way is perfect; the word of the Lord is tried* (now the word tried here means to be tested. In other words, God's word, God's Covenant was proven and found to be true)*: he is a* ***buckler*** *to all them that trust in him. '*

The word **buckler** means a small shield made for hand-to-hand fighting.

In other words, “as for God, His way is perfect; the word of the Lord is tried, He is a shield that will fight your battles. And not only fight your battles but allow you to triumph over your oppressors.

Ok you’ll get that later. Listen, if you see it in the word of God that means God’s word cannot come back void or in the form of a lie. God’s word has stood the test of time. And you can open the word of God and read for yourself how plagues, locust, life, death fire has possessed the land. And here we are again repeating the cycle because of the choices man had made.

Psalms 25:2 NLT - *'I trust in you; do not let me be put to shame, nor let my enemies' triumph over me. '*

Watch this, the book of Psalms has 150 love letters written to God’s people. And almost half of those letters are talking about the enemy. And these enemies are those who reject or oppose not only the children of God, but God’s law, which is the word of God.

That’s why the believers in this verse start this Praise off with,” I trust in you.” why because they know that the word is in God, and God is in the word and the word is God’s truth.

Psalms 25:2 KJV reads this way, *'O my God, I trust in thee: let me not be ashamed, let not mine enemies' triumph over me. '*

Now if we go back up to the first verse. It reads - *'Unto thee, O Lord, do I lift up my soul.* '**KJV**

David wrote this song to say, Lord I trust you so much that I dedicate my life back to you, why because only you know how to protect that which you've given me. Then David goes to say and while I am dedicating my life to you God, I need you to keep my enemies far from me. Help me to win against my enemies, help me to survive their cheap, immature tactics. I don't understand what they're thinking God. I'm not sure about their way reasoning, but I do understand this, I can't make it without you.

Lord Have Mercy!!!

We have to have enough sense to know that we cannot win against sin. We have to know that we can't survive on our own thinking. We cannot afford to depend on no one but God.
God Help Me.

Proverbs 3:5-6 KJV – *Trust in the Lord with all thine heart; and lean not to thy own understanding.*
'v6 In all thy ways acknowledge Him and He will direct thy path.

When it comes to making decisions in our lives, it is best to leave them up to someone who's been there already, who knows the ends and outs about business decisions, marriage, life, finance, love and so much more. It's important to let someone help lead, guide and direct you and do it all His name is Jesus.

April 2, 2020

For the last two months Amen, we have been in divine connection with God when dealing with the topic, "Having a peace of mind." I for one have been absolutely captivated and blown away on how God has taken His powerful yet patience time in helping us understand the word of God when dealing with the mind. And I don't know about you, but I am excited to see where God will lead us Hallelujah, in the next several weeks, or in the weeks to come when developing an understanding through the word of God of having a peace of mind.

And I know someone might say, well Pastor why are you excited, shouldn't you know or understand the subject before bringing the word before us?

And the answer is Yes, I'm excited because I can hardly wait at times to share with you what God has shown me, however, there are times when the Holy Ghost will reveal or answer a raised question, yours or mine as a matter of fact right in the mist of us.

So yes, I study to show myself approved unto God. And I might want to say one thing on a particular matter, but then the Holy Ghost will say, tell them this instead.

Alright, just felt like giving transparency really quick.

On last week, we left on a powerful high note of understanding the question, **what is trust?**
And the answer was revealed that **trust** is found Proverbs 3:6 In everything we do, we are to acknowledge and then allow God to lead and direct our path.

And I know someone is thinking, well Pastor I acknowledge God, I pray and talk to God, but I feel like in certain things I have to fix things on my own, I have to do this for myself. You have to understand, I've been doing this for myself, by myself and with myself for so long. I've been let down so many times before and I just feel like I can't afford to just let anybody in my space right now. My heart can't take another let down.

And on tonight, that's where we will start, on the heart.

In understanding the dynamics of having a peace of mind, there are so many things that falls under that topic or that title. Will we be able to reach and or cover them all? Afraid not, why, because I believe that God is allowing us to have some access to this subject to at least give us incite or an idea of the movement of God.

Meaning, there are certain things that are and will take place in and on the earth that God does not want His people to be ignorant about. And what do I mean by ignorant, I mean that God does not want us to be lost or not knowing what's going on around us. Amen.

For years unnumbered the Bible has been this beaker of light, this road map to destiny and grace by leading and directing us through the world's traps and turmoil. And when we are tried, it is not to see how well we standup through the test. It is to see how well our faith endorse throughout the test.

Listen, when we say or hear the cliché "My heart can't take this anymore" what we are actually saying or what we are hearing is, I'm not sure I can trust even God right now.

Listen to me, if you ever get to this point in life, stop what you are doing and find a prayer warrior that will help you through.

If and when you start thinking you can't trust God, you want to give up on life or you hate God, or you not talking to God. Get yourself under someone you DO trust, honor, respect and have them to pray you through.

The Pastor and Songwriter, Edward Mote wrote the lyrics to the song; "my hope is built on nothing less, but Jesus' blood and Righteousness. I dare not trust the sweetest frame, wholly lean on Jesus' name.

Now watch this here's my favorite part, "on Christ the solid rock I stand, all other ground is sinking sand."

When this world has tried her very best to pull us down, it will be nothing but the blood of Jesus that will lift us up. It will be nothing but the blood of Jesus that will keep our mind. It's nothing but the blood of Jesus that will keep our hearts in tune with His word.

God, I Feel Good Right There!!

Let's take a look at **Isaiah 63:17 KJV-** *'O Lord, why hast thou made us to err* (go astray; to fail) *from thy ways, and hardened our heart from thy fear* (to reference, to honor, to respect)? *Return for thy servants' sake, the tribes of thine inheritance. '*

Keep your finger there. And turn to
Exodus 9:12 KJV- *'And the Lord hardened the heart of Pharaoh, and he hearkened not unto them; as the Lord had spoken unto Moses. '*

These two scriptures indicate that God initiated the actions or the negative feelings behind these recipients. In no shape or form will God ever tell you hate me with all your heart

Scripture Reading:
Joshua 24:15 KJV - *'And if it seem evil unto you to serve the Lord, choose you this day whom ye will serve; whether the gods which your fathers served that were on the other side of the flood, or the gods of the Amorites, in whose land ye dwell: but as for me and my house, we will serve the Lord. '*

Isaiah 26:3 KJV - *'Thou wilt keep him in perfect peace, whose mind is stayed on thee: because he trusteth in thee. '*

6
Having a Peace of Mind Deliverance

April 9, 2020

As we dive into the next element of Having a Peace on Mind, which is Deliverance, please continue to go over the scriptures that the Lord has entrusted us with that we would apply them in our everyday living. We are made one with God and He is holding us accountable for the lessons we learn and how we learn and use these study guides in our daily walk.

I understand that we have been confined to the house for some time now and we feel like we are going to burst if we do not and do something.

Well, if by chance you must stick your head out of the door for few minutes. Begin to thank God for bringing you one more day. Take a minute to look around you and thank God for allowing you to be able to see what's going on around.

I think at times, we take God for granted for the little things that others would give their right arm for, such as sight, taste, touch, feel, being able speak, read, write, breathe. I mean the list goes on and on.

And on tonight it's my desire that we will be able to make a list of the things, experiences even people the Lord has actually delivered us from. And by composing this list, amen we will be able to see how much God loves and where God has brought us from.

So, the question that is presented tonight, **what is Deliverance?**

According to The New Combined Bible Dictionary written by Charles Pheiffer, the deliver is defined as to be set, redeemed or to be saved.

So right where you are, at this very moment, I want you to take 1 minute and write down as many things you can think of that God has brought you through, from, where God is taking you. Do that now.

Now as you look over your list and you see the places God has brought you from, you see the people He's blessed you to leave or they have left you, you see the jobs He denied you, you see the decisions He made you rethink. I MEAN COME HERE YOU GOT TO SEE WHAT GOD WAS AND IS DOING.

Lord Have Mercy.

It's obvious, or at least it should be. How God has allowed us in certain friendships, certain relationships Hallelujah to let you see that's not where I want you.
It should be obvious how God has allowed us to be placed on certain jobs for a period time. And we think that we were going to collect our 401K from this job, but God says I have something a whole lot better for you.

And sometimes we get mad, upset and angry with God because we want what we want when we want it.

Can I share this with you?

God will not ever withhold His Blessing from us, in fact He's waiting for us to get ourselves together so that He can Bless us. Praise the Lord.

When it comes to your freedom, let me tell you God does not play. He refuses to have bound, tied up or even strangled Praise the Lord by lives endeavors. Why do you think God took our sins and mistakes to the cross, so that no man could hold accountable for the past?

Which brings us to a place where our past sometimes is thrown in our faces Praise the Lord. And when that happens, it almost seems like the matter took place minutes ago, but God has resurrected us from that life Praise God. He has redeemed us from the yester years. That's why God won't allow certain friendships and relationships to work because He knew that if that friend, associate or lover ever gets mad enough, they would be quick to bring up what you use to do, where you use to go.
But I'm here to encourage you that God has the final say. And what God says, I called you into freedom.

Scripture Reading:

Lord Jesus, turn to **John 8:33-36 KJV- 33** *They answered him, we be Abraham's seed, and were never in bondage to any man: how sayest thou, Ye shall be made free?* ***34*** *Jesus answered them, Verily, verily, I say unto you, whosoever committeth sin is the servant of sin.* ***35*** *And the servant abideth not in the house for ever: but the Son abideth ever.* ***36*** *If the Son therefore shall make you free, ye shall be free indeed. '*

Jesus was talking to the believers, the descendants of Abraham. Jesus warned the people that if they sinned, they would be slaves to sin, but since the Son of God has already made provision to sets the people free from sin, then they should they are free indeed.

Now what does that mean?

Does that mean if I sin right now or does my past sins cause me to be a slave to sin?

Now before I answer that question, turn to:

James 4:17 KJV- *'Therefore to him that knoweth to do good, and doeth it not, to him it is sin.'*

James 4:17 NLT- *Remember, it is sin to know what you ought to do and them not do it.*

Here's the answer: Our past sins, our current sins and our future sins have all been forgiven when

Jesus died on the cross. Now, will Jesus continue to allow us to make the same mistakes?

Absolutely not. God will grow tired of the sins of the world, and this is primarily why we are where we are right now because of the choices man has made against God.

Scripture Reading:
Jeremiah 29:17 NLT - *'17This is what the Lord of Heaven's Armies says: "I will send war, famine, and disease upon them and make them like bad figs, too rotten to eat.* ***18****Yes, I will pursue them with war, famine, and disease, and I will scatter them around the world. In every nation where I send them, I will make them an object of damnation, horror, contempt, and mockery.*
19*For they refuse to listen to me, though I have spoken to them repeatedly through the prophets I sent. And you who are in exile have not listened either," says the Lord.'*

And here's where you will hear folks say I can't help myself or I can't stop doing it.

Matthew 6:13 KJV- *'And lead us not into temptation, but deliver us from evil: For thine is the kingdom, and the power, and the glory, for ever. Amen. '*

7
Having a Peace of Mind Getting Guidance, Direction & Instruction

April 16, 2020

Scripture Reading:

Exodus 23: 20-33; 24: 1-12. Psalms 32:8; Psalms 37:23; Psalms 121:8; Proverbs 3:5-6; Isa. 48:17; John 16:13 and Rev. 3:8

We will be dealing with several scriptures from the Bible that has already been solely designed to help us understand and recognize the need of following directions, especially those directions and instructions that come from the Lord.

It has been in my experience that when I make it a priority to follow directions to the letter, Amen, I am rewarded unmeasurably. Only because there is something that is greatly needed for me to do not for me personally, but for the Kingdom.

In other words, whatever Instructions that are and were given to you and to me, they must be completed for the sake of the assignment. And I am not saying that no one else can or cannot complete the assignment, but what I am saying is that we all have specific instructions that we must adhere to.

In order for us to remain in God's Will, we need to be obedient to the Instructions given to us and under no circumstances are we to try and complete our assignment and then try to finish someone else's work.

When we bite off more than what's required of us, we will soon find out that the assignment is no longer a(n) assignment but now the assignment is a mess.

Why? Because someone felt like that part of the assignment should have been assigned to them; according to who?

God gives the assignments and we have been set aside to do one thing and one thing only; fulfill it.

And whether the assignment is great or small is not the concern, it's how we fulfill that assignment is what matters.

Scripture Reading:
Proverbs 3:5-6 NLT – *5Trust in the Lord with all your heart; do not depend on you own understanding. 6Seek His will in all you do, and He will show you which path to take.*

I know some of us may feel like our idea is the best idea or our plan maybe the best plan, but keep in mind where the idea came and who gave it to you.

Listen, God doesn't need a run-away wagon jeopardizing what's been asked of us. And keep in mind that God doesn't need our help, but for lack of a better word the best way to help God is to get an understanding.

Then there are some of us who may feel that the directions are not clear when in actuality the instructions are so clear that they seem cloudy.

Have you ever received directions from someone, and you just knew that it was more to it than just that?

And you are left sitting there, waiting for the directions to be so complicated. And while the directions are being given, you're somewhere in your mind trying to get your thoughts together to see if you are even capable of completing that which has been ask of you to do. You are or have already counted yourself out because, you think the directions are unclear because they are straight to the point. Which then causes you to over think a situation, or over analyze a thing too much.

When I was in my earlier teens, my mom use to say to me, come and listen to my directions. Amen, after my mother gave me her instructions, she would always follow up with this one statement, "repeat them back to me." To make sure that I understood her instructions.

It was almost impossible to mess up the instructions, because the way they were given. However, if by chance those directions were not followed exactly, all I had to do was play back in mind what those directions were.

Now here's transparency, sometimes I was on point, other times I was not. The times I was on point, my mom would say, "Good Boy."

Those other times, she would send me back again with the same directions and wherever she was in the house, she would feed me those same directions over again until she knew that the job was done.

Well, that's just like God isn't it?

God gives us explicit instructions to follow in order to help us grow and these instructions comes from His word. The Bible is filled with instructions on how to fulfill every commission.

We, the Children of God must take the time to study God's word so that when instructions are given, we will know exactly what to do, when to do it, and how to do it. God's word is a road map to success. And when we allow the word of God to work with the Holy Spirit that lives down on the inside of us, we are destined for victory.

Is this an easy process, is this an easy road? Of course not, But with God on our side all things are possible we, just have to believe.

8
Having a Peace of Mind
Being in the Presence of God

April 23, 2020

Scriptures for Learning:

Gen. 3: 7-8; Exodus 14:19; Exodus 33: 14-15; Ezek. 36:26-27; Psalms 16:11; Matthew 28:16-20; Psalms 100:2; II Cor. 3rd Chapter and Lev. 22:3

On tonight we will take a look at a few scriptures in our continued learning in, "Having A Peace of Mind" that will give us some insight for our sub-topic of being in the presence of God. Please know that these are not all of the scriptures that deal with God's

Presence, but these are some of them that the Lord has shown me, as of right now.

Being in the presence of God doesn't mean that we have done anything great. Being in God's presence doesn't come from the gifts, the talents, the accomplishments that the Lord has granted us. Being in the presence of God is given only because He chose or He chooses to whom He wants to be in His presence, that's it.

Whoever the Lord feels like being in their presence, that's where He will be. And what that means, people shouldn't feel slighted, left out, betrayed or in their feelings, because God isn't in your space. He may be with me today and you tomorrow, no one knows that but God.

And just because we have a relationship with God, doesn't mean that He's in our presence. Because we are in a relationship with God, it means that we are covered by God. And we are going to talk about this tonight and more next week, I already feel it.

What is the Presence of God?

According to, "Eerdmans Dictionary of the Bible", the word **presence** is defined *as being in the face of God.*

We would want to always be in the presence of God or be in the face of God no matter what we've done, because while we are in the presence of God, we are made right with God.

Hallelujah

While we are in the face of God, we can admit our wrong to God, which is called repentance causing us to be redeemed (redeemed means to be set free) by God. But we try to hide from God, by the way, which is impossible to do, we become stagnated and soon to become lost, why because we respect our shamefulness more rather than fear God's Glory.

When we speak on God's Presence, we are speaking on God's placement.
Where is God?

God is Omnipresence, which means God is everywhere. God was and is there before we got there, and He never left from where He was. He's God!!

Listen IT. IS. IMPOSSIBLE to hide from God's presence.

Man has tried for decades to hide from God's Presence. Since the beginning of time, man has used countless efforts to avoid the all-knowing, all seeing and all-Powerful God.

What is Hiding from God's Presence?

God knew the intent of man's heart before man could even think about it. God already predicted the sin and made arrangements or a plan for escape even while in the sin.

When we try to hide and or reject God's Presence, when we try to hide from God's face, we are headed to a life of forever pain and damnation.

Let's take a look at **Genesis 3:7-8** – KJV *And the eyes of them both were opened, and they knew that they were naked; and they sewed fig leaves together and made themselves aprons.*

8And they heard the voice of the Lord God walking in the garden in the cool of the day: and Adam and his wife hid themselves from the presence of the Lord God amongst the trees of the garden.

Before the bite of the apple, Adam and Eve were ignorant or naïve to their authentic lifestyle. They knew nothing about their nakedness until after the sin was committed. You see it doesn't become sin until after the deed has been done. Yours, mines, our shamefulness does not become radioactive until we recognize what we've done. And when we recognize our error, we fall into a disgraceful state of being, because we feel as though that we have brought a discredit to who we are.

But can I share something with you?

When we fall short of God's word. And the world has taken advantage of us, it is then that God will come, He will step right into our mess and He will sooth all of our gilt, pain, disgrace, sin, both known and unknown. And He washed them away, how, by allowing us to be in, His Presence.

And someone maybe wandering, why would the Lord allow that to happen?

What folk don't understand, or overlook is, the Lord gave them instructions and both Adam and Eve forgot, ignored, didn't pay attention is not the point. The point is when we want to run and hide because of our mistake, God will be ever so present to cover us even our shame.

Turn to **Leviticus 22:3 – NLT** *Say to them: 'For the generations to come, if any of your descendants is ceremonially unclean and yet comes near the sacred offerings that the Israelites consecrate to the Lord, that person must be cut off from my presence. I am the Lord.*

We cannot continue to think that because we serve a loving, patience and forgiving God that He will constantly put up with sin. Falling short of God's word is completely different from ain't nothing going to happen to me type of attitude.

God says, I come with news that I always keep my promises. The good news is I come that you may have life and have it more abundantly, the bad news is when I tell you to department from for I know you not, that's where you will fall out of the Presence of God.

And God says, you see, because of my constant warnings that you've ignored, I've got to punish you. God says, I spent seconds, which to us would be days, months and sometimes years planning our future, but we still want to do things our way. And you're not tired yet of the shame that you are bringing yourself, your family or to me.

God says, I've got to punish you, by cutting you off from my Presence. And when someone has been cut from God's Presence, they have been cut from God's Favor, they have been cut from God's Grace and Mercy.

Listen, when you have been cut from God's Presence, you will soon feel like you're lost in a weary land. Where you once had things in your life locked down and to now see everything around you has become untied and falling apart.

Now, does that mean that we can never get back into the Presence of God? Well, that all depends on you. You knew what you went through to find God. And knew what it took for you to stay in God's Presence.

HAVING A PEACE OF MIND
SUB-TOPIC: BEING IN GOD'S PRESENCE Part2

April 30, 2020

Scripture Reading:

Gen. 3: 7-8; Exodus 14:19; Exodus 33: 14-15; Ezek. 36:26-27; Psalms 16:11; Matthew 28:16-20; Psalms 100:2; II Cor. 3rd Chapter and Lev. 22:3

On tonight we are on part 2 of **"Being in God's Presence"** under the topic **"Having a Peace of Mind."** On last week we covered, "what is the presence of God?" we also covered, "what is hiding from God's presence?"

And tonight, we will start off our class with, "How can I get in God's Presence?"
Amen

How can I get in the Presence of God?

The truth of matter is, it is not difficult to get in the Presence of God. The Presence of God is ALLLLLL Around Us, so to not think otherwise would be a grave mistake on our part. You see God's Presence or being in the Presence of God will allow us to know or sense He's there just like a spider sense.

I'm quite sure one time or another in your lives you've seen the television series, cartoon or movie, "Spiderman." This young man name Peter Parker, better known as Spiderman, was a college student and a regular born brain. One day Peter Parker was on a science trip with his class.

To make a long story short, a spider got caught up in this energy transfiguration in a chemistry lab. The spider landed on Peter's hand, refused to let him go and then it happens, the spider bit him. Moments later Peter didn't feel quite like himself; something had come over him. And after some time had passed, Peter started to feel better than ever before.

Keep in mind that when this spider bit Peter on the hand, the spider transferred its capabilities over to the young man. One of the characteristics of the spider is called a six sense. Being able to know when something is wrong, but not yet truly understand the danger.

Spiderman now has the capability to know when something is wrong. And that capability is called a spider sense. The spider sense gives the hero a heads up when danger is coming or near.

God, I hope I'm helping you tonight.

And see we are no different than Peter Parker. We may not have been born with a big brain, but we are the children of God which makes us wise as a serpent, but humble as doves. Oh, Praise the Lord.

And just like Peter something fell on us, something came over us. We might not have been bitten by a spider Praise the Lord, but something got a hold of us and refuse to let us go.

It's not by accident that Peter got these brand-new powers from the spider. It was purposed that Peter was at the right place at the right time.
It's not by accident that we, the children of God are in His Presence Praise the Lord. It was and is by God's designed; it was purposed that we were in the right place at the right time to find ourselves in the Presence of God.

So, the question tonight is, how can I get in the Presence of God?
I thought you figured it out by now, but we the children of God have to be in the right place at the right time.

Being in the right place and at the right time is crucial. Praise the Lord. And we need to be reminded that TIMING IS EVERYTHING Praise the Lord.

Ezekiel 36: 26-27 KJV - *A new heart also will I give you, and a new spirit will I put within you: and I will take away the stony heart out of your flesh, and I will give you an heart of flesh. 27 And I will put my spirit within you, and cause you to walk in my statutes, and ye shall keep my judgments, and do them.*

Ezekiel 36: 26-27 NLT *'And I will put my Spirit in you so that you will follow my decrees and be careful to obey my regulations. And I will give you a new heart, and I will put a new spirit in you. I will take out your stony, stubborn heart and give you a tender, responsive heart. '*

Praise the Lord. We the body of Christ must have a warm, compassionate, alive and receptive heart. Praise the Lord, in order to be in the Presence of God.

That's why **Psalms 95:2** it reads, *Let us come before his presence with thanksgiving and make a joyful noise unto him with psalms.*

Many times, people are afraid or have reservations about coming to God, because of their past Praise the Lord. They want to come to church without being judged because of their history. Praise the Lord.

And I just want to encourage someone tonight who maybe listening that your past has nothing to do with the Plan that God has on your future.

When you are ready to accept Christ as your Lover, then that's when your past will be cleansed by God's Blood. God will then transform your cold heartedness into a heart that He can work with.

Yes, God gave you the original heart, but see something happened along the way. And caused you to turn from God, but the good news is, God never turned away from us. We may not have seen Him or felt Him because of the hardness or shame from our hearts. And that's why God is saying here in Ezekiel 36 in order for me to use you, I've got to change you. In order for me to fit in your life, Praise the Lord, you've got to allow me to take somethings out.

God says I want to give you a heart that's light and not heavy. I want to give you a heart that's free and not burden down Praise the Lord.

And see here in Ezekiel chapter 36, Ezekiel had to encourage Israel that was going to keep His promise, but first God had to restore them back to a place where He could uproot them from the snares of darkness. And place them in area of receiving God's joy.

When we allow God the chance to bring us into a place of receiving divine favor, we will be in the Presence of God. And just Spiderman's spider sense watching out for him, God's Presence is watching out for us.

Therefore, causing our dreams to be manifested. In **Joel 2:28 KJV-** it reads, *And it shall come to pass afterward,* (after I've come into your life, Oh Praise the Lord, after I took out the old and replace it with a new, after I cleansed your past and placed promise on your future) *that I will pour out my spirit upon all flesh; and your sons and your daughters* (not just you, but all who are connected to you) *shall prophesy, your old men shall dream dreams, your young men shall see visions:*

You see when we allow God access to our broken and harden hearts, it is then that we can reap the benefits of God's Presence. Praise the Lord. We may not have spider senses Praise the Lord, but we have dreams and visions that God will increase and or maximize through our prophetic words. Praise the Lord.

HAVING A PEACE OF MIND
Being in God's Presence Part3

May 7, 2020

Scripture Reading:

Gen. 3: 7-8; Exodus 14:19; Exodus 33: 14-15; Ezek. 36:26-27; Psalms 16:11; Matthew 28:16-20; Psalms 100:2; II Cor. 3rd Chapter and Lev. 22:3

On tonight we are on part 3 of **"Being in God's Presence"** under the topic **"Having a Peace of Mind."** On week before last we covered, "what is the presence of God?" we also covered, "what is hiding from God's presence?"

On last week we were able to cover, "how to get in the Presence of God?"
And this week's bible study, we are covering the portion of Being in God's Presence, entitled, "When God Moves or the Movement of God." Praise the Lord

It is my desire that when we come together, that we are actually applying the rules and or the guidelines when it comes to Having a Peace of Mind.
Especially when it comes to being in God's Presence. Praise the Lord.

You see while we are in this mess up world, while we are dealing with our everyday trials and tribulations, rest assure that we are still covered by God's Presence.

Being in the Presence of God does more than just cover us Praise the Lord but being in the Presence of God causes God to move on our behalf. When something is happening in the earth or around us that doesn't seem or feel right. Causing us to sometimes get out of control, to lose focus, to scatter our thoughts wanting us to think that we can run away from the issue. But when we are in the Presence of God, it causes a spiritual chemistry that will alert God to take action on our behalf to ward off, fight or protect us from those.

Watch this, according to Webster's Dictionary 1828, the word **move** is defined as *to impel; to carry; to excite into action, to move with passion.*

God doesn't just move when we have our good days, Praise the Lord. God also moves during our not so good day too. Praise the Lord.

You're trying every day to be better than the day before. Seeking God's direction in life Praise the Lord.

And here comes the doorbell ringing while you're trying to study, the children or the spouse trying to break your praying time, someone trying to bring you gossip all while you are trying to get in the Presence. And see what these small distractions don't know or fail to remember, it is a bad place to be in the Presence of an angry and jealous God.

God knows your heart and He knows where you are trying to get to. And God doesn't want you to fight Praise the Lord. God will do the fighting for you. Praise the Lord.

We are the children of God and It's quite ok for you to tell those obstacles to be careful how you handle a child of the King.

That's why having a relationship with God is vital Praise the Lord, why because when the enemy sends his little emps and demons to trick and trap you, that's when God will take action on your behalf. Causing you to prosper and your enemies to fall. Praise the Lord. And not only will your enemies fail Praise the Lord. The Bible declares that you won't ever have to worry about them again. Lord Help!!!

I don't know about you, but I do know that God is still working on me Praise the Lord. I know that I'm growing in grace, because somethings that use to irritate me, I smile at now, why because in my mind I'm saying a quick prayer for God to come see about me.

In my mind I'm asking God to be quick to avenge me. I remind God; you said in your word that you are my rod and my staff. I remind God that you said you are my shelter in the time of need. And I am holding You accountable to your word.

Exodus 14: 13-14 KJV – *And Moses said unto the people, Fear ye not, stand still, and see the salvation of the Lord, which He will shew to you to day: for the Egyptians whom ye have seen to day, ye shall see them again no more for ever.*
The Lord shall fight for you, and ye shall hold your peace.

Here Moses had to remind and encourage God's people to not be afraid and or run from the enemy, Praise the Lord, but stand firm and watch God work on your behalf.

Moses had to encourage God's people that when you follow the Presence that He will keep you in perfect peace. Praise the Lord.

When the doorbell rings, the children, the spouse, and the gossipers come. God said to stand still and watch me work.

I'm here to encourage you, when these small meaningless things try to convert you back to place of doubt, fear, loneliness. When this world tries to betray you. I want you the children of God, to stand firm on God's word. Praise the Lord.

I want you to smile and start praying silently and watch God work. And while God is moving, I want you to stay in the peace of God, which is His Presence.

Isaiah 26:3 KJV – *Thou will keep him in perfect peace, whose mind is stayed on thee: because he trusteth in thee.*

9
Having a Peace of Mind When we Overcome the Powers of Darkness

May 14, 2020
Scripture Reading:
Rev. 12:11; Eph. 1:7; Psalms 107:2; 1John 1:7; Roman 5:9; Matthew 4: 1-11; II Cor. 5:21; Heb. 13:12; I Cor. 3:16; Psalms 81:9; II Cor. 6:14

The Lord has placed in my spirit that we all share a few things in common as a Holy Spirit led Church. And one of the things we all share is; How to do deal with and how to overcome the powers of darkness. Amen.

And you have to understand my dark time may not be like your dark time. We all have and or will face a season of going through that period of darkness. It is inevitable, we cannot escape it, we can't outrun it, and the truth is; that period of darkness will come. And the question that should be burning down within us is this:

What will we do when it comes?

My friends, when dealing with the powers of darkness; and its main objective which is constantly trying to overpower, overwhelm, overthrow and finally the ultimate goal is; to kill us.

Yes, we sometimes fall because of the design of which the darkness is and or was intended. In other words, the enemy knows the very person, place and or thing that we wish we could get rid of and or forget. And no matter how hard we try; darkness will use that to get us to repeat history instead of being reformed from history.

And we sometimes beat ourselves up more than the dark power could. Because we feel like we are so strong, or we are so saved. We feel like we're so anointed that this type of thing shouldn't be happening to us.

Well can I give you a quick reminder and or a word of encouragement?

We could never have a testimony if we are never tested. We could never tell the goodness of Jesus and all that He has done for us, if we aren't allowed to go through certain things. Praise the Lord.

Scripture Reading:
Let's look at **Matthew 4:1-11-KJV**

1.*Then was Jesus led up of the Spirit into the wilderness*
to be tempted of the devil. **2***And when he had fasted forty*
days and forty nights, he was afterward an hungered.
3*And when the tempter came to him, he said, If thou be*
the Son of God, command that these stones be made
bread. **4***But he answered and said, It is written, Man*
shall not live by bread alone, but by every word that
proceedeth out of the mouth of God. **5***Then the devil*
taketh him up into the holy city, and setteth him on a
pinnacle of the temple, **6***And saith unto him, If thou be*
the Son of God, cast thyself down: for it is written, He
shall give his angels charge concerning thee: and in
their hands they shall bear thee up, lest at any time thou
dash thy foot against a stone. **7***Jesus said unto him, It is*
written again, Thou shalt not tempt the Lord thy God.
8*Again, the devil taketh him up into an exceeding high*
mountain, and sheweth him all the kingdoms of the
world, and the glory of them; **9***And saith unto him, All*
these things will I give thee, if thou wilt fall down and
worship me. **10***Then saith Jesus unto him, Get thee*
hence, Satan: for it is written, Thou shalt worship the
Lord thy God, and him only shalt thou serve. **11***Then the*
devil leaveth him, and, behold, angels came and
ministered unto him.

Let us focus our attention on verses 1-4.

1.*Then was Jesus led up of the Spirit into the wilderness to be tempted of the devil.* **2***And when he had fasted forty days and forty nights, he was afterward an hungered.* **3***And when the tempter came to him, he said, If thou be the Son of God, command that these stones be made bread.* **4***But he answered and said, It is written, Man shall not live by bread alone, but by every word that proceedeth out of the mouth of God.*

If the Historical Jesus, better known as the Earthly Jesus, can be tempted by the enemy when Christ was in His weak state, why can't we?

You see, it is quite evident on how the enemy works. Think about it, he only pursues when we become or on the verge of becoming weak.

Here the devil pursued Jesus when He got weak due to hunger. And you know it's the devil working when he tries to get you to justify the act. The devil tempted or better yet dared Jesus, if you are the Son of God, then turn these rocks into bread.

And Jesus with His anointed, smooth and sophisticated self, told the enemy even while in His weakened condition, "*Man shall not live by bread alone, but by every word that proceedeth out of the mouth of God.*"

In other words, Jesus decided not to use His power to change the rocks into bread. Why? He remembered

God's word in **Genesis 50:21** *Therefore do not be afraid. I will provide for you.*

And I won't lie to you, the devil has been telling me you know you want another piece of pie. And the next time you get piece, put a little butter pecan ice cream on top. And I answer him, you know that sounds like a good idea.

Watch this, weakness doesn't become weakness until we act on the weakness. I'll say it again, weakness doesn't become weakness until we act on the weakness. It was my love for ice-cream that caused me to get in the car (pre-meditated), drive to the market, get out of the car, walk in the market, go to the frozen foods, look for my favorite kind (breyer's), get in line, pay for the ice-cream, get back in my car, drive back home, wash my hands, crack the seal, get the spoon and bowl. I mean the weakness goes on and on.

Listen, I realize that some of us are in a tight fix right now. And we feel like there is no way out but, let me cover you in prayer with this. He who the Son set free, is free indeed. God knew and knows all about our time of need. And the Bible says, He is quick to answer. That means before you begin to pray, God is already working it out for your good. As a matter of fact; God has already worked it out. We just have to believe and trust the will and the favor of God that is on our lives.

Let's go to verses 5-8

5*Then the devil taketh him up into the holy city, and*
setteth him on a pinnacle of the temple, **6***And saith unto*
him, If thou be the Son of God, cast thyself down: for it
is written, He shall give his angels charge concerning
thee: and in their hands they shall bear thee up, lest at
any time thou dash thy foot against a stone. **7***Jesus said*
unto him, It is written again, Thou shalt not tempt the
Lord thy God.

When the enemy is not satisfied or is so desperate to prove a point, he will stop at nothing to shake our faith. His slick words again came after Jesus. Listen to what he says, "if you are the Son of God, go ahead and jump, don't worry God will send angels to help you."

Hear me, I believe this is where the spirit of suicide is birth. When people feel like all is lost, feel like they don't have anything to live for. And some would even deposit more of the enemy's language into their thinking by speaking phrases like: I wish I could end it all, no one really loves me, no one is going to miss me anyway, I wish I were never born. These are the seeds that were and are planted in the mind.

And someone right now reading this book, yes, you, I believe that you are seeking answers to questions that no one seems to be able to help you with. My brother, my sister, allow me to encourage you right now.

You are on the verge of receiving the full blessing of God. I speak life over you; I speak healing over you, I speak abundance of joy and deliverance over you right now.

I don't know who you are, but I speak the strength that God gave Samson, I speak the Favor of God that was given to Moses and I speak the wisdom and the financial relief that God gave Solomon, In Jesus Name.

Surround yourself with Positive, Anointed, Praying, God Fearing People; so that when times like these try to consume you, they will know exactly how to move on your behalf under the instructions of the Holy Ghost.

I know you sit and wander to yourself, why are these things happening to me, why isn't God answering my prayers, what did I do to deserve this?

Well, God always has a plan and there will be times when we do not and will never understand the plan of God, but this one thing is for sure; God promised us in His word in Hebrews 13:5 He said, *"... I will never leave you nor forsake you."* And I don't know if you have trust issues or not, but I'll tell you like my mom tells me, "When God writes the check, you can be sure that it will always clear."

When things of uncertainty arise, when things pop up, “out of the blue,” out of order or unbalanced it’s usually done to the fact that just around the corner lies your breakthrough. Just a few more yards away is your relief, your miracle, your blessing is waiting for you. How?

Look at verse 7. Jesus said unto him, “*It is written again,”* I already told you one time, but see your head is hard “*Thou shalt not tempt the Lord thy God.”* I have a breakthrough, I do not have, nor will I ever have a breaking point. I have a breakthrough. And My breakthrough is Christ Jesus. My way out; is Jesus. My deliverance; is Jesus. My healing; is Jesus.

Come on let’s keep going. I told you I’m trying to teach, I’m trying to teach, Praise the Lord.

Let’s look at verses 8-11

8Again, the devil taketh him up into an exceeding high mountain, and sheweth him all the kingdoms of the world, and the glory of them; 9And saith unto him, All these things will I give thee, if thou wilt fall down and worship me. 10Then saith Jesus unto him, Get thee hence, Satan: for it is written, Thou shalt worship the Lord thy God, and him only shalt thou serve. 11Then the devil leaveth him, and, behold, angels came and ministered unto him.

WHEN WE OVERCOME THE POWERS OF DARKNESS part2

May 21, 2020

Amen, as we continue our second encounter with overcoming the powers of darkness, I want you to consider the thought of what it would be like if we did not have a Warrior like the Lord.

Our lives would be dysfunctional without the Master.

Yes, there are somethings in our lives that we wish could change, but if we think about it, I mean really think about it. And after we thought it and came to the conclusion, that if it had not been for the Lord on our side, Praise the Lord, where in the world would we be?

GOD HELP!!

Folk walk around day after day without at least acknowledging God. They don't thank God for allowing them to see a new day, you know, they are that brazen where they think that it wasn't God who woke them up this morning, Praise the Lord.

Folk go to restaurants, drive thru or worst, they pull up to the dinner table and begin to devour their meal without first thanking God for the food. You hear by word of mouth or see on the news and social media, how the enemy has plotted and planted these perverse thoughts in the minds of the food caregivers to do all kinds of disrespectful things to your food. And you have the audacity to swallow the food without at least thanking God first, so that He can cover the food as it goes down into your digestive system. Praise the Lord

I'm reminded of a story about a woman in her youth Praise the Lord who was strong, smart, funny, a hard worker, Amen, but she was also a prankster, you know someone who loved to laugh and make others laugh. Amen.

This young lady would even have fun joking her neighbors, Amen. And I wish I had the time to tell the whole story but let me get to my point. I shared with you earlier how the enemy would try anything to get inside of your mind by plotting and planting these perverse thoughts in others to get to you.

And that's exactly what happened to this funny and smart girl. The neighbor had cooked their dinner and placed it in the window seal to cool. This young lady thought it would be funny to take and eat the neighbor's food. After the young lady had taken the food and ate it, the story goes on that sometime later the young lady started to not to feel so good. Praise the Lord.

They tell me that this smart and funny girl had been poisoned by the food that the neighbor had left in the window.

I hope you catch this; you see when you do not have a relationship with God, you are made venerable, you are left uncovered from God's protection that will allow you to be subjected to almost any form of attack, Praise the Lord. And you see, I believe that neighbor had been under the attack of the enemy, why because no one but the devil could have come up with a more diabolical plan to enable the life of another. The mere thought of you coming up with such a deed should have made the average person sick to their stomach to even think of a thing.
But hear me, when you are under the watchful eye of the Almighty God, there is nothing that the enemy can do to get rid of you.

The young lady didn't die, Praise the Lord but for the rest of this young lady's life had been changed.

Lord Help!!

Once a substance is in your system Amen, or once there is an unrecognizable object that has been ingested into your body. You will start to feel all kinds of the wrong thing Praise the Lord, causing your white and red blood cells to work overtime to try to fight off any parasites that has engulfed your body.

Why are you sharing this Pastor?

I want you to fully understand that the devil is not playing with you. And he will use any means necessary to impede your progress. The enemy sees you trying to grow, and he will stop at nothing to get you to stop, even if it's to infect someone close to you to get to you. Praise the Lord.

That's why it should be a part of your diet to read God's word every day, so that not only your mind can stay sharp and covered, but your Spirit man is ready to fight off any demonic parasites that may come.

Let's take a look at **I Cor. 3:16 & 17 KJV-** *'Know ye not that ye are the temple of God, and that the Spirit of God dwelleth in you?*

If any man defile the temple of God, him shall God destroy; for the temple of God is holy, which temple ye are.

Paul was sent to advise the Corinthian church that their bodies are the temple of the Lord's. And they cannot allow to have anything, or anyone come in and TRY to disrupt the temple of God. Let me put it to you this way. You see our bodies, our minds, and our very being do not belong to us. And people seem to have this false perception that these bodies belong to them, where we can do anything we want with and or to them. And the truth of the matter is, we cannot.

God lent us these bodies for one purpose and one purpose only, to do His Will. Praise the Lord. And when we add for a better word these artificial flavors to the body, we are tainting or staining the temple of God.

God, I wish I had time to teach this thing, you see the word artificial means its man-made, its fake, fabricated, Lord Help it's a substitute for the real thing. It doesn't come directly from the natural source for which something was intended.

Watch this, according to the "Journal of The Royal Society of Medicine", the plant called Nicotiana was first discovered by Columbus back in the 1800's. This plant was used as a herb to help with certain ailments in its original form. However, after man found a way to alter the intent in the which the plant was created for. Instead of it being a help aide, it has been tampered with to become a fix. And it is now the leading killer of over 3 million people worldwide called Nicotine, better known as cigarettes, cigars, snuff, chewing tobacco and so on.

And when we allow this quick fix, backyard remedies to be introduced to our bodies, it is now considered a substitute for the real thing.

Well, what is the real thing?
Haven't you been listening?

The real thing is called the Holy Spirit. And just make sure we understand, the Holy Spirit is not a thing where we pick up and now and then to get a quick fix Praise the Lord. The Holy Spirit is a person, that lives down on the inside of us leading and guiding and directing our footsteps.

And God says, because My Spirit lives in you, He is charged to defend that body at all cause.

Well Pastor, how come Johnny's body wasn't protected from him smoking weed? or
How come Jessica's body wasn't protected from her drinking alcohol?

Listen, the devil has many forms to trap us and drag us into his world. Some of us get caught up in the rat race and some of us manage to escape, but the truth is we all have a choice.
Joshua 24:14-15... choice

Now is it ever too late to reject or get rid of the substance(s) that is trying to make a home in your body? The answer is No!!

But what if I've been smoking, drinking, using drugs, living a lifestyle that's not pleasing to God for so long? And!

God wants us to make an effort, meaning even when you begin to think that you can do better that's when the Holy Spirit will take over. Never forget that the Holy Spirit lives inside of you. He will never leave you, even if we begged Him Praise the Lord, He will never leave you. Believe it or not, but you're stuck with God.

And when you make up in your mind that you want a peace of mind, that's when God says it's about time. God knows it's a process to be completely healed and delivered from an addiction. And please don't be limited to the basic addictions of drugs, alcohol and smoking, because there're addictions that people may have that only God knows about and only God can deliver them from it.

But when you take the initial first step, by telling God you don't want this in your life, that's the beginning stage of healing.

Go to **Psalms 81:9 KJV -** *There shall no strange god be in thee; neither shalt thou worship any strange god.*

David is saying that you can speak in the atmosphere yourself and declare Victory over yourself. When you speak in the world or in the atmosphere of things you want or things you don't want. God has assigned Angles to each of us to hear those words and act on them.

Whatever the parasite that is trying so hard to latch on to you, I want you to speak these words, "Therefore there shall no strange god be in me." And keep saying it until that parasite has left you.

You see, and I'm going back to a lesson we already had. It was the same for Jesus when He was tempted by the enemy while He was going through. And after so many attempts, Jesus told the devil to get behind Him. And after Jesus spoke the enemy left Him.

Now please know this that the enemy has seasons to move. Meaning the enemy has been removed from you for a minute, but he can return. And it's ok, while he's gone, we have to keep fighting by praying and fasting and reading God's word to keep our minds from all form of darkness.

WHEN WE OVERCOME THE POWERS OF DARKNESS part3

May 28,2020

Scriptures for Learning

Rev. 12:11; Eph. 1:7; Psalms 107:2; 1John 1:7; Roman 5:9; Matthew 4: 1-11; II Cor. 5:21; Heb. 13:12; I Cor. 3:16; Psalms 81:9; II Cor. 6:1-14

On tonight we are working on our 3rd series of Overcoming the powers of darkness under our main topic, Having a peace of mind. It is my desire that God reveals the scriptures to me Amen, so that you will be endued with power to overcome those soon to come, if not already here challenges. Amen

Three weeks ago, or so, when the Lord shared with me that in order for God's people to have a peace of mind, they will have to encounter some things. Amen, and whatever those things are and or were, weren't the problem. The problem was that some of God's people, not all, but some of God's people would or will not know how to overcome darkness when it does come. Praise the Lord.

And so, God has given me permission, Praise the Lord to share with the body of Christ on how to or what to do when darkness tries to peak and stick his malicious hands where it doesn't belong. Praise the Lord.

As we move along life and we think that all is well because nothing is going wrong, all around us is good. Be careful about that because somewhere along the road darkness is lying patiently waiting for just the right time to attack.
You see it is the natural order of a lion to stay low in the shrubs and to get as close as he possibly can to his prey, amen so when the attack comes, there is no way for an escape. Praise the Lord.

Not only that, but when these deceivers, manipulators, these unbelievers try to get us to join their methodology, amen, their way of thinking. You now, want us to agree that the sky is plaid and not blue. Trying to convince us that there is no God, Lord Help. Trying to pretend to be your friend so that they can get all in your business and try to exploit you later if you don't agree to be their friend.

And we the children of God, have to stay alert of these kinds of thinkers, why? because they are quick to change and or alter the minds of the naive. Praise the Lord. Now please keep in mind that the word naïve has nothing to do with babes in Christ or those who are new to the body of Christ, because a slick talker can get almost anybody, amen.

But if we the children of God are using or exercising our gift of discernment like we should, then we wouldn't fall for almost anything, amen.

And I share this word with you because I want you to be armed at all times. It is my pray that the Blood of Jesus illuminates and overwhelms you so much so that it doesn't leave room for darkness.

And here in II Corn. The 6th chapter, amen Paul had been recruited by God to warn but yet encourage the Corinthian Church to be careful to not mix righteousness with wickedness, amen to be sure to stay away from those who were practicing an unholy lifestyle.

Paul asked the Corinthians a question. The question posed to the people was, how can light live with darkness?

Amen, and that's where we will start, turn to II Corn. the 6th chapter and let's start with verses 1-2.
II Cor. 6:1-2- KJV- *We then, as workers together with him, beseech you also that ye receive not the grace of God in vain. (For he saith, I have heard thee in a time accepted, and in the day of salvation have I succoured thee: behold, now is the accepted time; behold, now is the day of salvation.)*

Here in verses 1 and 2 of the 6th chapter in the book of 2nd Corinthians, Paul not only encourages the people of God, but he begged them that as they work together or partner together with God, to not reject the grace that God had given them, as well to not take God's word for granted either.

God even told the Corinthian Church that while you are going through your dark place, while you are going through your dark time that this is the right time to help you before you make mistake.

And God is doing that right now for some of us, we are about to make a mistake like never before. We've been getting the signs; we've ignored the warnings and we still want to do things our way. And God is saying now is the time for me to step in, now is the time for me to rescue again before we get into something, we won't be able to get out of.

You know folk have a hard time dealing with what's real and what's make believe. False prophets and fortune tellers going around telling you to play 1234 and you'll win big. Now don't yawl go play that number because I'm going to ask God to cancel it, Amen.

False teachers, witches and fortune tellers try to fill your mind with false doctrine, but God say my word will not come back void. God says I come that you might have life and that you will have life more abundantly, Praise the Lord.

Amen, look at verses 3-13
II Corn. 6:3-5 KJV- *Giving no offence in any thing, that the ministry be not blamed: But in all things approving ourselves as the ministers of God, in much patience, in afflictions, in necessities, in distresses, In*

stripes, in imprisonments, in tumults, in labours, in watchings, in fastings;
By pureness, by knowledge, by longsuffering, by kindness, by the Holy Ghost, by love unfeigned, By the word of truth, by the power of God, by the armour of righteousness on the right hand and on the left, By honour and dishonour, by evil report and good report: as deceivers, and yet true; As unknown, and yet well known; as dying, and, behold, we live; as chastened, and not killed; As sorrowful, yet alway rejoicing; as poor, yet making many rich; as having nothing, and yet possessing all things. O ye Corinthians, our mouth is open unto you, our heart is enlarged. Ye are not straitened in us, but ye are straitened in your own bowels. Now for a recompence in the same, (I speak as unto my children,) be ye also enlarged. '

Paul is saying here that as Ministry for Christ go on. And we the believers continue to trust in the work of the Lord; we will all be faced with challenges. We will all be tested of our faith. To see if wavering to the left or to the right is any good.
Being in the body of Christ doesn't mean that life will get better, being in the body of Christ means that we will be strengthen so that life can be better.

What we go through as Christians or Believers can never kill us Praise the Lord why because God will never put on us too much that we can't bare it.

Folk always praying and asking God; Lord please don't let me go through this or Lord I don't know why I have to go through that.
It is while we are in that dark place that God will give us grace and He will get the Glory.

Turn to **II Corn 12:9 KJV** - *And he said unto me, my grace is sufficient for thee: for my strength is made perfect in weakness. Most gladly therefore will I rather glory in my infirmities, that the power of Christ may rest upon me.*

You see when we find ourselves in that dark place, trying so desperately to get out. Begging and pleading with God to remove it and trying to rebuke it will not bring you peace. The only peace you will receive while going through is when God whispers that still voice, "My Grace is sufficient.

While we are in our weakest moment, God says I'll give you peace right in the mist of the storm. You see whatever storm that may try to form, God's strength overpowers that dark moment. When you are ready to throw in the towel. When you say enough is enough, God say's my Grace is enough for you to push through that dark time.

In other words, my Sister and Brother, you have the power within you to push through the pain, push past the hurt, and push through the suffering. God says, My Grace rules over every disappointment. When infirmities and opposition come up against you, speak God's Grace in the atmosphere. And you will literally see the Hand of God trample over every enemy (whatever that's not like God) in your life.

You see the enemy has no power, especially over the Children of God. When you are a child of the king, you are a part of a Royal Priesthood. You come from good stock. Praise the Lord. And there is nothing that your Heavenly Father won't do to keep and protect His own.

Yes, we will all face some form of adversity, but the good news is, we have and serve an All-Powerful God.

Turn to **I Peter 2:9 – KJV-** *But ye are a chosen generation, a royal priesthood, an holy nation, a peculiar people; that ye should shew forth the praises of him who hath called you out of darkness into his marvellous light:*

No matter what darkness tries to come, it is God's Marvelous Light that will always overpower the power of darkness. Why because you a are child of the Most-High God. You were chosen to go through some things in order for you to get God's Grace and Glory.

10
Having a Peace of Mind

Fear Doesn't Live Here Anymore

June 11, 2020
Scriptures for Learning:
Psalms 23:4, Psalms 27:1, Psalms 34:4, Isa. 41:10, Matt. 28:20, II Thess. 3:3, II Tim. 1:7 and I John 4:18.

Let's deal with the hard, cold facts that no one likes fear or to be afraid of anything and or anyone. It doesn't feel good and doesn't look good when others can see fear on your face when you are confronted by an adversary.

I remember one family reunion trip we went on; I believe we were in Myrtle Beach. Anyway, my oldest niece, Dynasty was much younger at the time and I want to say that she was about 5 or 6. My family and I went to this theme park or a boardwalk of some sort that had a haunted house.

To make a long story short, Dynasty saw the house and was afraid so much that she didn't want me to go in. I tried to encourage her, I said, "It's going to be alright; I'm coming right back." But the look on her face told me that she didn't believe a word I just said. From the time we went in the haunted house until the time we returned, Dynasty would not stop crying, because she just knew something was going to happen to me.

I must admit by looking at the exterior of the haunted house, it was not a pretty sight and the inside was far worse. The haunting and creepy music started to play as we were wheeled in.

Not knowing what to expect, we all clung to each other just to make sure we weren't separated. Objects of all kinds were popping out in your face or something and or someone was touching you on the shoulder. I believe we were more afraid of being on the inside than little Dynasty being afraid on the outside.

When we finally exited from the haunted house, Dynasty ran and jumped into my arms. I reassured again her, "that it was all over and there was nothing to be afraid of." She held on to me so tightly, as to say I'm never letting you go again.

What am I saying?

Sometimes when we see and or hear things that we just don't quite understand or are unfamiliar with, it could cause one to have some form of fear.

And one or two things will generate from such an experience. One, the fear of something will consume us so much so that we will begin to believe what that illusion is trying to predict. In essence causing one to become fretful, to panic, being overwhelmed, and sometimes causing one to have anxiety.

According to Dictionary.com, **fear** is defined as: <u>A distressing emotion aroused by impending danger, evil,</u>

pain, etc., whether the threat is real or imagined; the feeling or condition of being afraid.

My Sisters and Brothers, believe it or not, fear has a father, and his name is Satan. And his only will in life is to kill, steal and destroy anything and anyone divinely connected to Jesus Christ. You can always tell the Will of God from the will of the enemy. The will of the enemy (through fear) will have you doubting yourself; and through that doubt forcing you to be in a(n) confused state of mind.

The trick of the enemy (through a false imaging, false statement and false or unclear gestures) will have you thinking that your spouse is stepping out on you.

The trick of the enemy (through the spirits of jealousy, envy and vengeance) will have you to think that everyone is against you, that no one cares or loves you. And after you have played and replayed the incident in your mind after so many times, the lie that the enemy has planted in your thought process now starts to feel, look, taste and sound like the truth.

God Help Us!!

And now you are left wondering what in the world happened? How in the name of God did I get here?

But there's good news. YOUR FAITH!!

Your Faith, which comes from The Will of God wants, needs and desires that we live in Perfect Peace. It is through the Will of God that we do not fear, but instead keep the Faith.

Fear causes one to live in imprisonment, but the Faith of God causes us to be set Free.

Watch this. Fear, I believe has a back door. Fear will either force you to become stronger whereas you've made up in your mind to have Faith in Christ and never allow anything or anyone to ever place you in this position of fear ever again.

Another way to identify fear. Fear deals with darkness. Have you ever noticed in almost every horror film 9 times out 10 the boogeyman via (male or female) now a days, always attacks their victims at night?

It seems like the nighttime or the darkness gives the boogeyman power over their prey. It's in the dark where things get confusing, and you begin to wander and hopelessly running off in the wrong direction.

Sounds familiar doesn't it?

But God would never allow us into uncertain dangers or allow us to go through certain situations where there was no way out. When we, the Children of God are faced with these nighttime challenges, we all but need to declare two words, Lord Help.

Scripture Reading:
Isaiah 41: 10 ***NLT*** – *Don't be afraid, for I am with you. Don't be discouraged, for I am your God. I will strengthen you and help you. I will hold you up with my victorious right hand.*

God knows the craftiness of the enemy. He knows that the enemy will try his best to lure God's people into unchartered territory to try and separate us from the Powerful Protection of the Almighty God.

Here in Isaiah 41 God makes it crystal clear that there is no way possible that the enemy could ever pull us from the Powerful and Righteous Hand of God. When we made the choice to turn our lives over to Jesus Christ, we were made in agreement that we will trust Him, and He would provide.

Throughout all your endeavors, I pray God will give you the Peace that passes all of your understanding.

This book has become so much more than what I anticipated. Why? because for several weeks God has been pressing me to teach a series on, Having a Peace of Mind.

I struggled with this assignment because I too had been going through so much in my own life. You name it I probably experienced it or know of someone who has. From dealing with the challenges of my new Pastoral Assignment to dealing with the jealousy of family and friends.

Not realizing that minutes, days, and weeks prior to charge that's been given to me God's people have been going through all forms of obstacles that would challenge their faith.

And I am so grateful that God has chosen and instilled in me a little piece Haven that can be used to encourage, restore, revive, and rebuild those who have been torn, scorned and rebuked; just to name a few. And He entitled it, "Having a Peace of Mind."

Lionel Pearson serves as the Senior Pastor at Regeneration Worship Center located right here in Charm City Baltimore.
Lionel Pearson is anointed Preacher and Teacher of God's word.
Pastor Pearson is not only an Author, but he's also the owner, operator and radio host of the podcast, Restor'd Radio.
Lionel Pearson is a Songwriter, Producer and Gospel Recording Artist.
Lionel Pearson and his wife, Katrina have a desire to see the love and the power of God manifest in the lives of His people.

Be Encouraged, know that I Love You

Lionel B. Pearson

www.ingramcontent.com/pod-product-compliance
Lightning Source LLC
LaVergne TN
LVHW020511100826
845148LV00003B/758

* 9 7 8 1 7 3 7 3 5 7 5 0 6 *